AF261203

THE PALACE OF UNBEARABLE FEELING

Anne Riesenberg

LILY POETRY REVIEW BOOKS

Published by Lily Poetry Review Books
223 Winter Street
Whitman, MA 02382

https://lilypoetryreview.blog/

ISBN: 978-1-957755-15-1

 Published in the United States by Lily Poetry Review Books.
Library of Congress Control Number: 2023930410

Cover photograph: Anne Riesenberg

Table of Contents

Form was not born from an idea. It was an idea vanishing.   — Cecilia Vicuña

THE PALACE OF UNBEARABLE FEELING

into this body this light into this body this light into this body this light into this body this light into this body this light
this body this light into this body this light into this body this light into this body this light into this body this light into
body this light into this body this light into this body this light into this body this light into this body this light into this
this light into this body this light into this body this light into this body this light into this body this light into this body
light into this body this light into this body this light into this body this light into this body this light into this body this
into this body this light into this body this light into this body this light into this body this light into this body this light
this body this light into this body this light into this body this light into this body this light into this body this light into
body this light into this body this light into this body this light into this body this light into this body this light into this
this light into this body this light into this body this light into this body this light into this body this light into this body
light into this body this light into this body this light into this body this light into this body this light into this body this
into this body this light into this body this light into this body this light into this body this light into this body this light
this body this light into this body this light into this body this light into this body this light into this body this light into
body this light into this body this light into this body this light into this body this light into this body this light into this
this light into this body this light into this body this light into this body this light into this body this light into this body
light into this body this light into this body this light into this body this light into this body this light into this body this
into this body this light into this body this light into this body this light into this body this light into this body this light
this body this light into this body this light into this body this light into this body this light into this body this light into
body this light into this body this light into this body this light into this body this light into this body this light into this
this light into this body this light into this body this light into this body this light into this body this light into this body
light into this body this light into this body this light into this body this light into this body this light into this body this
into this body this light into this body this light into this body this light into this body this light into this body this light
this body this light into this body this light into this body this light into this body this light into this body this light into
body this light into this body this light into this body this light into this body this light into this body this light into this
this light into this body this light into this body this light into this body this light into this body this light into this body
light into this body this light into this body this light into this body this light into this body this light into this body this
into this body this light into this body this light into this body this light into this body this light into this body this light
this body this light into this body this light into this body this light into this body this light into this body this light into
body this light into this body this light into this body this light into this body this light into this body this light into this
this light into this body this light into this body this light into this body this light into this body this light into this body
light into this body this light into this body this light into this body this light into this body this light into this body this
into this body this light into this body this light into this body this light into this body this light into this body this light
this body this light into this body this light into this body this light into this body this light into this body this light into
body this light into this body this light into this body this light into this body this light into this body this light into this
this light into this body this light into this body this light into this body this light into this body this light into this body
light into this body this light into this body this light into this body this light into this body this light into this body this
into this body this light into this body this light into this body this light into this body this light into this body this light

is   is
is there   there is
is there an   an there is
is there an image   image an there is
is there an image of   of image an there is
is there an image of thriving   thriving of image an there is
is there an image of thriving that   that thriving of image an there is
is there an image of thriving that does   does that thriving of image an there is
is there an image of thriving that does not   not does that thriving of image an there is
is there an image of thriving that does not depend   depend not does that thriving of image an there is
is there an image of thriving that does not depend on   on depend not does that thriving of image an there is
is there an image of thriving that does not depend on success on depend not does that thriving of image an there is
                                             success
                                             success
                                             success
is there an image of thriving that does not depend on success on depend not does that thriving of image an there is
is there an image of thriving that does not depend on   on depend not does that thriving of image an there is
is there an image of thriving that does not depend   depend not does that thriving of image an there is
is there an image of thriving that does not   not does that thriving of image an there is
is there an image of thriving that does   does that thriving of image an there is
is there an image of thriving that   that thriving of image an there is
is there an image of   of image an there is
is there an image   image an there is
is there an   an there is
is there   there is
is   is
is there   there is
is there an   an there is
is there an image   image an there is
is there an image of   of image an there is
is there an image of thriving   thriving of image an there is
is there an image of thriving that   that thriving of image an there is
is there an image of thriving that does   does that thriving of image an there is
is there an image of thriving that does not   not does that thriving of image an there is
is there an image of thriving that does not depend   depend not does that thriving of image an there is
is there an image of thriving that does not depend on   on depend not does that thriving of image an there is
is there an image of thriving that does not depend on success on depend not does that thriving of image an there is
                                             success
                                             success
                                             success
is there an image of thriving that does not depend on success on depend not does that thriving of image an there is
is there an image of thriving that does not depend on   on depend not does that thriving of image an there is
is there an image of thriving that does not depend   depend not does that thriving of image an there is
is there an image of thriving that does not   not does that thriving of image an there is
is there an image of thriving that does   does that thriving of image an there is
is there an image of thriving that   that thriving of image an there is
is there an image of   of image an there is
is there an image   image an there is
is there an   an there is
is there   there is
is   is

it is important to break down the notion of failure
it is important to break **down the notion of failure**
it is important to **break down the notion** of failure
it is **important to break** down the notion of *failure*
it is important to **break** down **the notion** of failure
it is important **to break down** the notion of failure
it **is important to** break down **the notion** of failure
it is important to break down the notion **of failure**
it **is important to break** down the notion of failure
it is important **to break down the notion** of failure
it is important to break down the notion of failure
it is **important to** break down **the notion of failure**
it **is** important **to break down** the notion of failure
it is important **to break** down the notion of failure
it is important to break down **the notion** of failure
it **is** important to break down the notion of ***failure***
it is important **to break down** the notion of failure
it is important to break down **the notion** of failure

birds build nests in every country birds build nests in every country
build nests in every country birds build nests in every country birds
nests in every country birds build nests in every country birds build
in every country birds build nests in every country birds build nests
every country birds build nests in every country birds build nests in
country birds build nests in every country birds build nests in every
birds build nests in every country birds build nests in every country
build nests in every country birds build nests in every country birds

nests in every country birds every country birds build
in every country birds country birds build nests
every country birds birds build nests in
country birds build build nests in every
birds build nests in in every country
build nests in every in every country birds
nests in every country birds every country birds build

in every country birds build nests in every country birds build nests
every country birds build nests in every country birds build nests in
country birds build nests in every country birds build nests in every
birds build nests in every country birds build nests in every country
build nests in every country birds build nests in every country birds
nests in every country birds build nests in every country birds build
in every country birds build nests in every country birds build nests
every country birds build nests in every country birds build nests in
country birds build nests in every country birds build nests in every
birds build nests in every country birds build nests in every country

.......lonely......lonely......lonely......lonely......lonely......lonely.......
..........as......as......as......as......as......as......as......as......as..........
........survival......survival......survival......survival......survival........
......lonely.....lonely......lonely......lonely......lonely......lonely.......
..........as......as......as......as......as......as......as......as......as..........
........survival......survival......survival......survival......survival........
......lonely.....lonely......lonely......lonely......lonely......lonely.......
..........as......as......as......as......as......as......as......as......as..........
........survival......survival......survival......survival......survival........
......lonely.....lonely......lonely......lonely......lonely......lonely.......
..........as......as......as......as......as......as......as......as......as..........
........survival......survival......survival......survival......survival........
......lonely.....lonely......lonely......lonely......lonely......lonely......
..........as......as......as......as......as......as......as......as......as..........
........survival.....survival......survival......survival......survival........
......lonely.....lonely......lonely......lonely......lonely......lonely.......
..........as......as......as......as......as......as......as......as......as..........
........survival......survival......survival......survival......survival........
......lonely.....lonely......lonely......lonely......lonely......lonely.......
..........as......as......as......as......as......as......as......as......as..........
........survival......survival......survival......survival......survival........

advocate for the unseen advocate for the unseen advocate for the unseen
for the unseen advocate for the unseen advocate for the unseen advocate
the unseen advocate for the unseen advocate for the unseen advocate for
unseen advocate for the unseen advocate for the unseen advocate for the
advocate for the unseen advocate for the unseen advocate for the unseen
for the unseen advocate for the unseen advocate for the unseen advocate
the unseen advocate for the unseen advocate for the unseen advocate for
unseen advocate for the unseen advocate for the unseen advocate for the
advocate for the unseen advocate for the unseen advocate for the unseen
for the unseen advocate for the unseen advocate for the unseen advocate
the unseen advocate for the unseen advocate for the unseen advocate for
unseen advocate for the unseen advocate for the unseen advocate for the
advocate for the unseen advocate for the unseen advocate for the unseen
for the unseen advocate for the unseen advocate for the unseen advocate
the unseen advocate for the unseen advocate for the unseen advocate for
unseen advocate for the unseen advocate for the unseen advocate for the
advocate for the unseen advocate for the unseen advocate for the unseen
for the unseen advocate for the unseen advocate for the unseen advocate
the unseen advocate for the unseen advocate for the unseen advocate for
unseen advocate for the unseen advocate for the unseen advocate for the
advocate for the unseen advocate for the unseen advocate for the unseen
for the unseen advocate for the unseen advocate for the unseen advocate
the unseen advocate for the unseen advocate for the unseen advocate for
unseen advocate for the unseen advocate for the unseen advocate for the

ONLY YOU
MY LOVE
CAN DECIDE
WHAT TO DO
WITH YOUR
ONCE AGAIN
INVISI BILITY
ONLY YOU
MY LOVE
CAN DECIDE
WHAT TO DO
WITH YOUR
ONCE AGAIN
INVISI BILITY
ONLY YOU
MY LOVE
CAN DECIDE
WHAT TO DO
WITH YOUR
ONCE AGAIN
INVISI BILITY
ONLY YOU
MY LOVE
CAN DECIDE
WHAT TO DO
WITH YOUR
ONCE AGAIN
INVISI BILITY
ONLY YOU
MY LOVE
CAN DECIDE
WHAT TO DO
WITH YOUR
ONCE AGAIN
INVISI BILITY
ONLY YOU
MY LOVE
CAN DECIDE
WHAT TO DO
WITH YOUR
ONCE AGAIN
INVISI BILITY
ONLY YOU
MY LOVE
CAN DECIDE
WHAT TO DO
WITH YOUR
ONCE AGAIN
INVISI BILITY
ONLY YOU
MY LOVE
CAN DECIDE
WHAT TO DO
WITH YOUR
ONCE AGAIN
INVISI BILITY

the feeling of feeling how you actually **feel** actually you how feeling of feeling the

the feeling of feeling how you **actually feel actually** you how feeling of feeling the

the feeling of feeling how **you actually feel actually you** how feeling of feeling the

the feeling of feeling **how you actually feel actually you how** feeling of feeling the

the feeling of **feeling how you actually feel actually you how feeling** of feeling the

the feeling **of feeling how you actually feel actually you how feeling of** feeling the

the **feeling of feeling how you actually feel actually you how feeling of feeling** the

the feeling of feeling how you actually feel actually you how feeling of feeling the

the **feeling of feeling how you actually feel actually you how feeling of feeling** the

the feeling **of feeling how you actually feel actually you how feeling of** feeling the

the feeling of **feeling how you actually feel actually you how feeling** of feeling the

the feeling of feeling **how you actually feel actually you how** feeling of feeling the

the feeling of feeling how **you actually feel actually you** how feeling of feeling the

the feeling of feeling how you **actually feel actually** you how feeling of feeling the

the feeling of feeling how you actually **feel** actually you how feeling of feeling the

approaching the capacity to speak freely
approaching the capacity to speak freely
approaching the capacity to speak freely
approaching the capacity to speak freely
approaching the capacity to speak freely
approaching the capacity to speak freely
approaching the capacity to speak freely
approaching the capacity to speak freely
approaching the capacity to speak freely
approaching the capacity to speak freely
approaching the capacity to speak freely
approaching the capacity to speak freely
approaching the capacity to speak freely
approaching the capacity to speak freely
approaching the capacity to speak freely
approaching the capacity to speak freely
approaching the capacity to speak freely
approaching the capacity to speak freely
approaching the capacity to speak freely
approaching the capacity to speak freely
approaching the capacity to speak freely
approaching the capacity to speak freely
approaching the capacity to speak freely
approaching the capacity to speak freely
approaching the capacity to speak freely
approaching the capacity to speak freely
approaching the capacity to speak freely
approaching the capacity to speak freely
approaching the capacity to speak freely
approaching the capacity to speak freely
approaching the capacity to speak freely
approaching the capacity to speak freely
approaching the capacity to speak freely

10

SELF- - -other- - -SELF- - -other- - -SELF- - -other- - -SELF
self- - -OTHER- - -self- - -OTHER- - -self- - -OTHER- - -self
SELF- - -OTHER- - -SELF- - -OTHER- - -SELF- - -OTHER
self- - -other- - -self- - -other- - -self- - -other- - -self- - -other
SELF- - -other- - -SELF- - -other- - -SELF- - -other- - -SELF
self- - -OTHER- - -self- - -OTHER- - -self- - -OTHER- - -self
SELF- - -OTHER- - -SELF- - -OTHER- - -SELF- - -OTHER
self- - -other- - -self- - -other- - -self- - -other- - -self- - -other
SELF- - -other- - -SELF- - -other- - -SELF- - -other- - -SELF
self- - -OTHER- - -self- - -OTHER- - -self- - -OTHER- - -self
SELF- - -OTHER- - -SELF- - -OTHER- - -SELF- - -OTHER
self- - -other- - -self- - -other- - -self- - -other- - -self- - -other
SELF- - -other- - -SELF- - -other- - -SELF- - -other- - -SELF
self- - -OTHER- - -self- - -OTHER- - -self- - -OTHER- - -self
SELF- - -OTHER- - -SELF- - -OTHER- - -SELF- - -OTHER
self- - -other- - -self- - -other- - -self- - -other- - -self- - -other
SELF- - -other- - -SELF- - -other- - -SELF- - -other- - -SELF
self- - -OTHER- - -self- - -OTHER- - -self- - -OTHER- - -self
SELF- - -OTHER- - -SELF- - -OTHER- - -SELF- - -OTHER
self- - -other- - -self- - -other- - -self- - -other- - -self- - -other
SELF- - -other- - -SELF- - -other- - -SELF- - -other- - -SELF
self- - -OTHER- - -self- - -OTHER- - -self- - -OTHER- - -self
SELF- - -OTHER- - -SELF- - -OTHER- - -SELF- - -OTHER
self- - -other- - -self- - -other- - -self- - -other- - -self- - -other

IMAGINE
RADICAL
VITALITY
IMAGINE
RADICAL
VITALITY
IMAGINE
RADICAL
VITALITY

^^^ENTER^^^THE^^^PALACE OF UNBEARABLE^^^FEELING^^^
^^^PALACE^^^OF UNBEARABLE FEELING^^^ENTER^^^
^^^PALACE^^^OF^^^UNBEARABLE FEELING^^^ENTER^^^
^^^UNBEARABLE^^^FEELING ENTER^^^THE^^^PALACE^^^
^^^UNBEARABLE^^^FEELING ENTER THE^^^PALACE^^^
^^^FEELING^^^ENTER^^^THE PALACE OF^^^UNBEARABLE^^^
^^^ENTER^^^THE^^^PALACE OF UNBEARABLE^^^FEELING^^^
^^^PALACE^^^OF UNBEARABLE FEELING^^^ENTER^^^
^^^PALACE^^^OF^^^UNBEARABLE FEELING^^^ENTER^^^
^^^UNBEARABLE FEELING ENTER THE^^^PALACE^^^
^^^UNBEARABLE^^^FEELING ENTER THE^^^PALACE^^^
^^^FEELING^^^ENTER^^^THE PALACE OF^^^UNBEARABLE^^^
^^^ENTER^^^THE^^^PALACE OF UNBEARABLE^^^FEELING^^^
^^^PALACE^^^OF UNBEARABLE FEELING^^^ENTER^^^
^^^PALACE^^^OF^^^UNBEARABLE FEELING^^^ENTER^^^
^^^UNBEARABLE^^^FEELING ENTER^^^THE^^^PALACE^^^
^^^UNBEARABLE^^^FEELING ENTER THE^^^PALACE^^^
^^^FEELING^^^ENTER^^^THE PALACE OF^^^UNBEARABLE^^^
^^^ENTER^^^THE^^^PALACE OF UNBEARABLE^^^FEELING^^^
^^^PALACE^^^OF^^^UNBEARABLE^^^FEELING^^^ENTER^^^
^^^PALACE^^^OF^^^UNBEARABLE FEELING^^^ENTER^^^
^^^UNBEARABLE FEELING ENTER THE^^^PALACE^^^
^^^UNBEARABLE^^^FEELING ENTER THE^^^PALACE^^^
^^^FEELING^^^ENTER^^^THE PALACE OF^^^UNBEARABLE^^^
^^^ENTER^^^THE^^^PALACE OF UNBEARABLE^^^FEELING^^^
^^^PALACE^^^OF UNBEARABLE FEELING^^^ENTER^^^
^^^PALACE^^^OF^^^UNBEARABLE FEELING^^^ENTER^^^
^^^UNBEARABLE FEELING ENTER THE^^^PALACE^^^
^^^UNBEARABLE^^^FEELING ENTER THE^^^PALACE^^^
^^^FEELING^^^ENTER THE PALACE OF UNBEARABLE^^^
^^^ENTER^^^THE^^^PALACE OF UNBEARABLE^^^FEELING^^^

a- - -body- - -will- - -utter- - -a- - -body- - -will- - -utter- - -a- - -body- - -will- - -utter
body- - -will- - -utter- - -a- - -body- - -will- - -utter- - -a- - -body- - -will- - -utter- - -a
will- - -utter- - -a- - -body- - -will- - -utter- - -a- - -body- - -will- - -utter- - -a- - -body
utter- - -a- - -body- - -will- - -utter- - -a- - -body- - -will- - -utter- - -a- - -body- - -will
a- - -body- - -will- - -utter- - -a- - -body- - -will- - -utter- - -a- - -body- - -will- - -utter
body- - -will- - -utter- - -a- - -body- - -will- - -utter- - -a- - -body- - -will- - -utter- - -a
will- - -utter- - -a- - -body- - -will- - -utter- - -a- - -body- - -will- - -utter- - -a- - -body
utter- - -a- - -body- - -will- - -utter- - -a- - -body- - -will- - -utter- - -a- - -body- - -will
a- - -body- - -will- - -utter- - -a- - -body- - -will- - -utter- - -a- - -body- - -will- - -utter
body- - -will- - -utter- - -a- - -body- - -will- - -utter- - -a- - -body- - -will- - -utter- - -a
will- - -utter- - -a- - -body- - -will- - -utter- - -a- - -body- - -will- - -utter- - -a- - -body
utter- - -a- - -body- - -will- - -utter- - -a- - -body- - -will- - -utter- - -a- - -body- - -will
a- - -body- - -will- - -utter- - -a- - -body- - -will- - -utter- - -a- - -body- - -will- - -utter
body- - -will- - -utter- - -a- - -body- - -will- - -utter- - -a- - -body- - -will- - -utter- - -a
will- - -utter- - -a- - -body- - -will- - -utter- - -a- - -body- - -will- - -utter- - -a- - -body
utter- - -a- - -body- - -will- - -utter- - -a- - -body- - -will- - -utter- - -a- - -body- - -will
a- - -body- - -will- - -utter- - -a- - -body- - -will- - -utter- - -a- - -body- - -will- - -utter
body- - -will- - -utter- - -a- - -body- - -will- - -utter- - -a- - -body- - -will- - -utter- - -a
will- - -utter- - -a- - -body- - -will- - -utter- - -a- - -body- - -will- - -utter- - -a- - -body
utter- - -a- - -body- - -will- - -utter- - -a- - -body- - -will- - -utter- - -a- - -body- - -will
a- - -body- - -will- - -utter- - -a- - -body- - -will- - -utter- - -a- - -body- - -will- - -utter
body- - -will- - -utter- - -a- - -body- - -will- - -utter- - -a- - -body- - -will- - -utter- - -a
will- - -utter- - -a- - -body- - -will- - -utter- - -a- - -body- - -will- - -utter- - -a- - -body
utter- - -a- - -body- - -will- - -utter- - -a- - -body- - -will- - -utter- - -a- - -body- - -will
a- - -body- - -will- - -utter- - -a- - -body- - -will- - -utter- - -a- - -body- - -will- - -utter
body- - -will- - -utter- - -a- - -body- - -will- - -utter- - -a- - -body- - -will- - -utter- - -a
will- - -utter- - -a- - -body- - -will- - -utter- - -a- - -body- - -will- - -utter- - -a- - -body
utter- - -a- - -body- - -will- - -utter- - -a- - -body- - -will- - -utter- - -a- - -body- - -will

(   ) untouched (   ) untouched (   ) untouched (   ) untouched (   )
(   ) your (   ) palm (   ) your (   ) palm (   ) your (   ) palm (   )
(   ) is (   ) no (   ) is (   ) no (   ) is (   ) no (   )
(   ) longer (   ) longer (   ) longer (   ) longer (   ) longer (   )
(   ) my (   ) cup (   ) my (   ) cup (   ) my (   ) cup (   )
(   ) reservoir (   ) reservoir (   ) reservoir (   ) reservoir (   )
(   ) trumpet flower (   ) trumpet flower (   ) trumpet flower (   )
(   ) volcano (   ) volcano (   ) volcano (   ) volcano (   )
(   ) untouched (   ) untouched (   ) untouched (   )
(   ) your (   ) palm (   ) your (   ) palm (   )
(   ) is (   ) no (   ) is (   ) no (   )
(   ) longer (   ) longer (   ) longer (   )
(   ) my (   ) cup (   ) my (   ) cup (   )
(   ) reservoir (   ) reservoir (   )
(   ) trumpet flower (   ) trumpet flower (   )
(   ) volcano (   ) volcano (   )
(   )

can you acknowledge how much has been lost due to your own misperceptions
can you acknowledge how much has been lost due to your own misperceptions
can you acknowledge how much has been lost due to your own misperceptions
can you acknowledge how much has been lost due to your own misperceptions
can you acknowledge how much has been lost due to your own misperceptions
can you acknowledge how much has been lost due to your own misperceptions
can you acknowledge how much has been lost due to your own misperceptions
can you acknowledge how much has been lost due to your own misperceptions
can you acknowledge how much has been lost due to your own misperceptions
can you acknowledge how much has been lost due to your own misperceptions
can you acknowledge how much has been lost due to your own misperceptions
can you acknowledge how much has been lost due to your own misperceptions
can you acknowledge how much has been lost due to your own misperceptions
can you acknowledge how much has been lost due to your own misperceptions
can you acknowledge how much has been lost due to your own misperceptions
can you acknowledge how much has been lost due to your own misperceptions
can you acknowledge how much has been lost due to your own misperceptions
can you acknowledge how much has been lost due to your own misperceptions
can you acknowledge how much has been lost due to your own misperceptions
can you acknowledge how much has been lost due to your own misperceptions
can you acknowledge how much has been lost due to your own misperceptions
can you acknowledge how much has been lost due to your own misperceptions
can you acknowledge how much has been lost due to your own misperceptions
can you acknowledge how much has been lost due to your own misperceptions
can you acknowledge how much has been lost due to your own misperceptions
can you acknowledge how much has been lost due to your own misperceptions
can you acknowledge how much has been lost due to your own misperceptions
can you acknowledge how much has been lost due to your own misperceptions
can you acknowledge how much has been lost due to your own misperceptions
can you acknowledge how much has been lost due to your own misperceptions
can you acknowledge how much has been lost due to your own misperceptions
can you acknowledge how much has been lost due to your own misperceptions
can you acknowledge how much has been lost due to your own misperceptions
can you acknowledge how much has been lost due to your own misperceptions
can you acknowledge how much has been lost due to your own misperceptions
can you acknowledge how much has been lost due to your own misperceptions
can you acknowledge how much has been lost due to your own misperceptions
can you acknowledge how much has been lost due to your own misperceptions
can you acknowledge how much has been lost due to your own misperceptions
can you acknowledge how much has been lost due to your own misperceptions
can you acknowledge how much has been lost due to your own misperceptions
can you acknowledge how much has been lost due to your own misperceptions
can you acknowledge how much has been lost due to your own misperceptions
can you acknowledge how much has been lost due to your own misperceptions
can you acknowledge how much has been lost due to your own misperceptions
can you acknowledge how much has been lost due to your own misperceptions
can you acknowledge how much has been lost due to your own misperceptions

WHAT'S LOST IS LOST WE ARE AT A LOSS WE ARE IN THE RED
LOST IS   WE ARE AT A   WE ARE IN THE RED WHAT'S
IS   WE ARE AT A LOSS WE ARE IN THE RED WHAT'S
          WE ARE AT A   WE ARE IN THE RED WHAT'S   IS
WE ARE AT A LOSS WE ARE IN THE RED WHAT'S   IS LOST
ARE AT A   WE ARE IN THE RED WHAT'S LOST IS   WE
AT A   WE ARE IN THE RED WHAT'S   IS LOST WE ARE
A LOSS WE ARE IN THE RED WHAT'S   IS LOST WE ARE AT
          WE ARE IN THE RED WHAT'S LOST IS   WE ARE AT A
WE ARE IN THE RED WHAT'S   IS LOST WE ARE AT A LOSS
ARE IN THE RED WHAT'S LOST IS   WE ARE AT A   WE
IN THE RED WHAT'S   IS LOST WE ARE AT A LOSS WE ARE
THE RED WHAT'S LOST IS   WE ARE AT A   WE ARE IN
RED WHAT'S   IS LOST WE ARE AT A LOSS WE ARE IN THE
WHAT'S LOST IS LOST WE ARE AT A   WE ARE IN THE RED
          IS LOST WE ARE AT A LOSS WE ARE IN THE RED WHAT'S
IS   WE ARE AT A LOSS WE ARE IN THE RED WHAT'S LOST
LOST WE ARE AT A   WE ARE IN THE RED WHAT'S LOST IS
WE ARE AT A LOSS WE ARE IN THE RED WHAT'S   IS LOST
ARE AT A   WE ARE IN THE RED WHAT'S LOST IS LOST WE
AT A   WE ARE IN THE RED WHAT'S   IS LOST WE ARE
A LOSS WE ARE IN THE RED WHAT'S LOST IS   WE ARE AT
          WE ARE IN THE RED WHAT'S   IS LOST WE ARE AT A
WE ARE IN THE RED WHAT'S   IS LOST WE ARE AT A
ARE IN THE RED WHAT'S LOST IS   WE ARE AT A LOSS WE
IN THE RED WHAT'S LOST IS   WE ARE AT A LOSS WE ARE
THE RED WHAT'S   IS LOST WE ARE AT A LOSS WE ARE IN
RED WHAT'S   IS LOST WE ARE AT A LOSS WE ARE IN THE
WHAT'S LOST IS   WE ARE AT A   WE ARE IN THE RED

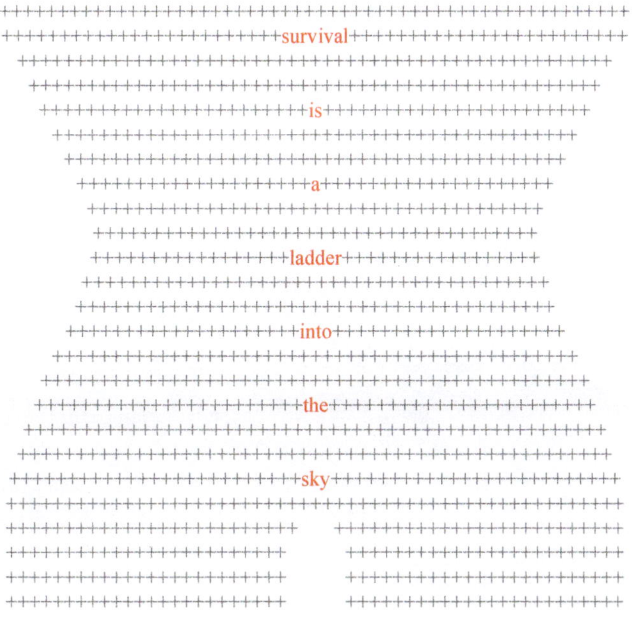

17

HOW
DO
YOU
LIVE
WITH
YOUR
SELF

Acknowledgements

The poems "lonely as survival" and "a body will utter" were previously published in *Voices Amidst the Virus*. "untouched" and "can you acknowledge how much has been lost" were previously published in *The Lily Poetry Review*. "only you my love can decide what to do with your once again invisibility" is the last line in a poem previously published in *The New Guard BANG!*

Special thanks to Eileen Cleary, Martha McCollough and Lily Poetry Press for their generosity, creativity, and literary stewardship.

To Andrea Read, Danielle Legros Georges, Susan Lewis, Alex Johnson, Katarina Weslien, Lauren Fensterstock, Shoshannah White and Jones Franzel, much love and appreciation for the insights and support that helped bring this work to fruition. The conversations about what inspires us and what we make have been invaluable.

To my brother-in-law Dan for his rigorous fidelity to what matters.

To Andy for his unwavering companionship and affection during difficult times, and Eleanor for being always herself, my deepest gratitude and love.

About the Author

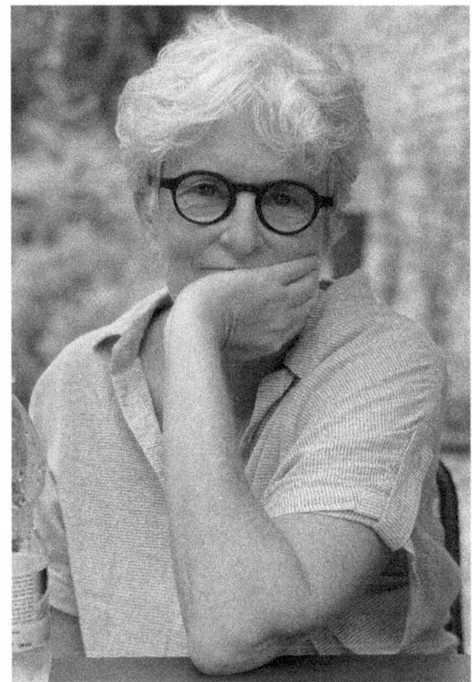

Photo by Andrew Graham

Anne Riesenberg is a writer, photographer and Five-Element acupuncturist living in Newcastle, Maine. A Pushcart and Best of the Net nominee, her work can be found in *Pleiades, Rogue Agent, Posit, Heavy Feather Review, The New Guard's BANG!, What Rough Beast* and elsewhere. Winner of Blue Mesa Review's Nonfiction and Storm Cellar's Force Majeure contests, she holds an MFA from Lesley University.

www.ingramcontent.com/pod-product-compliance
Lightning Source LLC
Chambersburg PA
CBHW042054030726
47599CB00019B/2487